FROM EMPLOYEE TO ENTREPRENEUR

The Journey is Real

JEWEL D. KITKO, MHA, CLSSGB, CHTS-IM

Self-Published 2018 | Florida, United States
Copyright © 2018 Jewel D. Kitko
All rights reserved. No part of this book may be reproduced in any form or by any electronic or mechanical means – except in the case of brief quotations embodied in articles or reviews – without written permission from its author.

ISBN 978-1729494141
Fort Lauderdale, FL

Table of Content

	Acknowledgments	I
	Introduction	1
1	The Entrepreneurial Journey Requires a Mindset	3
2	The Entrepreneur's Principal Mindset	6
3	The Employee's Perspective and Self-Discovery	10
4	Research – Plan, EIN and D&B Number	17
5	Research – Target Audience	21
6	Research – Social Media Influencers	26
7	Research - Vendors, Innovation & Stability	31
8	Research – Competitors as Resourceful Rivals	36
9	Product, Service Selection and Pricing	49
10	Invest in Yourself and Your Legacy	51
11	Negatives and Positives to Being an Entrepreneur	56
12	Rinse and Repeat Entrepreneurial Journey Q&A	60
	Conclusion	65

Acknowledgments

To my Son. my Why, **Chad Nicholas Kitko**. You have made me stronger, better and more fulfilled than I could have ever imagined. I am honored, privileged and blessed to be both your Mom and Grandmother to your beautiful children **James "Jack"** and **Sasha**.

To my Pillar, my heart and soul and the love of my life, **Jesse Billy Thompson**. Thank you for your unconditional love and support; and keeping me grounded, focused, and standing in faith, as walking away was NOT an option!

Introduction

We have all heard the terms *"be entrepreneurial"*, *"entrepreneurship"*, *"be an entrepreneur"*, *"move from employee to entrepreneur"* - they all sound great. They all sound like being your own boss will put you at the top of the world and there will be no issue. But I want you to understand that when you decide to transition from being an employee to starting your business is a journey.

For many it is a journey of empowerment. In many instances it is a journey of rise and fall and in the midst of it all, some will find success. But at the end of the day, you should know that the path to fulfil your entrepreneurial dreams is not an overnight success – *it is a journey*. There will be bumps and bruises on the road, and if I am being honest with you, being an entrepreneur is not for everyone!

Here's the deal - without the proper strategic planning and execution, your entrepreneurial dreams can rise and fall in a New York minute. If you are an online entrepreneur your social media page content and followers will wither away. It is important to plan and execute effective if you want to continue your vision of purpose for your legacies.

I am the Founder and CEO of Diamond HIT Consult LLC. My role as a certified Health-IT Implementation Manager has provided successful results in both private physician and ambulatory practices. These results support the restructure and transition from a paper-based to an electronically innovative operations of efficiency.

I am committed to serving as a health services executive leader. My passion and purpose are to mentor upcoming and transitional entrepreneurs, to live a healthy and balanced life by applying ethical principles to every area of their lives. My inspiration came about when I recognized that there was a need for the work I offered. I was knowledgeable about the services provided, and what it took to support and provide these services.

But, that being said, I also needed to keep a roof over my head. So, I did what had to be done. I made a game changing move. I needed to work on a stronger foundation, without any what-ifs. I knew that as an employee at any point in time, and any quarter, it could all come to an end. That simply wasn't going to work for me, nor the clients I serve.

I trust you will also find the inspiration and passion as an entrepreneur from my experience and the information that I will share in this book.

CHAPTER 1

The Entrepreneurial Journey Requires a Mindset

In this book, we will define the Employee to Entrepreneur journey and the impact of confidence-building throughout that journey. This will include the pitfalls and lessons learned as you determine your true purpose, passion, and platform.

At the foundation of entrepreneurship is a mindset as to the way you think and act. It is envisioning innovative ways to solve problems and create value in the market place. Ultimately, entrepreneurship is about the ability to recognize, methodically analyze opportunities, and to also capture its value.

As you go on this journey it is vital to balance a resilient vision with a disposition to embrace change. The ability to effectively listen to the views of clients or staff members, is also vital to your success. Having the confidence to make your own decisions is significantly important as well.

However, do not become too detached from the target market and staff members' needs to which you will primarily serve.

Entrepreneurship is the ability to visualize the bigger picture, discover the primary opportunities to make the clients' present state better, design concepts surrounding those opportunities, and continually validate such theories.

Initially and routinely, you will find yourself in a state of trial and error. Some tests will work; yet many will fail. It is not a journey of big exits, substantial net worth or living a glamourous life. It takes hard work, tough skin and tenacity. After all you are leaving what seems like the safe and protect environment of the workplace to embark upon uncertainty.

The ability to identify countless possibilities in every circumstance is critically important; there will be endless challenges that will test your hustle and grind. Successful entrepreneurship requires perseverance.

The most driven and successful entrepreneurs have never given up on their ideas. When challenges occur – and they sure will with you as well - they had to tap into innovative resources to overcome such events.

Aspiring and existing entrepreneurs must be able to adapt to the fluctuating economic states; and embrace innovative technology advancement, to maintain and increase client engagement. These are critical factors that contribute towards to your business goals.

Entrepreneurship involves a mindset that permits you to see opportunities universally. This could be a business conception that also includes recruiting industry leaders and subject matter experts that can help excel you're your business platform.

CHAPTER 2

The Entrepreneur's Principal Skillsets

As you embark upon this employee to entrepreneur journey, there are some principal skillsets that you must possess. In this chapter, I share with you those skillsets that every entrepreneur should have.

Be Resilient

Be resilient with the ability to withstand the highs and lows of business, as there is no fool-proof, cookie-cutter method that proceeds exactly the way the business plan outlines it. This is a skillset that empowers the entrepreneur to keep moving forward no matter the outlook .

Be Focused

Once you have define your long term vision and mission for your business, you must remain focused in order to meet your goals. Discover how to "laser focus" on each step in order to get closer to your ultimate goals. There are numerous expected and unexpected distractive forces as you build a business, so it is important to point out that this skillset may be a challenge to master.

Invest in Yourself and Your Business

This is particularly important for both the short and long-term periods. Most entrepreneurs are impatient and focus only on current state or next event, opposed to the appropriate direction to meet their business operational needs.

Now I know this might be a tough pill to swallow, but overnight success can take 5 to 10 years. In fact, it is going to be important to get your act together within the first five years as the IRS may determine that your business is just a hobby. Through the process of building in those initial years, entrepreneurs need to pause, revise/reposition and plan on a quarterly basis for more accurate assessment.

Locate and manage staff

This will include identifying talent for your business that may offer their service virtually. Make sure you understand how to leverage your employees, vendors and other resources so that you can build an expandable and innovative business.

It is going to crucial that you invest in networking with like-minded individuals, because you cannot achieve these steps on your own. As an entrepreneur you want to strive to authentic and timely feedback from all these resources.

Promotion and Marketing

As an employee, this was a skillset you did not necessarily need unless you worked in that specific department. However as you own boos and operator of your business you must -whether you want to or not - launch and sustain a promotion and marketing campaign to ensure long-term success.

Entrepreneurs are consistently needing to promote and market their ideas, products or services to existing and prospective customers and target market, investors or staff. The promotions run on a specific schedule and time zone, when existing and prospective customers and target markets are canvassing social media and ready to purchase.

Ideally, social media venues provide analytic tools, so entrepreneurs can monitor the viewers' comments, reactions, shares and engagement on the promotions; including which products and service responses were high and initiated sales or needed to be pulled and revised.

Educate yourself and your staff

Successful entrepreneurs recognize they do not have all the answers and their industry is constantly evolving. Entrepreneurs stay informed on new hardware, software, technology facets, and industry trends. Treat this process as if you are interviewing for a position or conducting a discovery meeting with a prospective client; of which you will need to come prepared with both questions and answers. You have to position yourself as the expert on the subject matter that concerns your business.

Self-reflection

A time of self-reflection will give you the opportunity to reflect on the past, current and future goals for an entrepreneur's personal and professional development areas. Continuously "in the grind" only leads to burnout on a physically and emotionally level for both the entrepreneur and the teams they lead.

Self-reliance

This is a MUST, even though there may be a plethora of phenomenal resources and support for the entrepreneur, in the end, entrepreneurs need to be beyond resourceful enough to depend on ourselves.

CHAPTER 3

The Employee's Perspective and Self-Discovery

As an employee, you normally set the tone across your organization; and play the role as an advocate for a charismatic workplace. Your role can also set you apart from other co-workers competing for the same area of expertise; including recognition in the industry.

You strive every day to ensure your organization has a positive, well-defined brand image that is clearly conveyed to your existing leadership. Your clients and co-workers also work diligently to leverage operational areas that attract exceptional industry-leading talent, maintain success and build revenue. It is a supported team effort, governed by a hierarchy of leadership.

The clear distinction of becoming an entrepreneur, is that you are defining your goal, purpose and passion, and platform launches. The success or failure of your pursuits now lie with you.

Picture it---you are now the business owner, CEO, founder and the entrepreneur that sets the platform to establish that hierarchy of leadership. You are now the one who basically sets the tone and advocates for the business. You hold the cards to where it all begins, thrives, struggles, and recovers. It starts with a mindset and vision and you are the one with it.

For the 9-5'ers, college students or those returning or transitioning to entrepreneurship, let me share some key excuses many of us use today. I was also guilty of this in my start-up phase.

Steer away from the *ifs*. They could basically end your goals before you even get started. I could become an entrepreneur *if* I had the money. *If* I had the education. *If* I had the resources. *If* I had better equipment. *If* I had the existing and prospective customers and target market. *If* I knew how to navigate through social media. The *ifs* will bury you.

How about turning the *ifs* into a positive statements? Besides, there will always be an *if*. Imagine you had the money, the existing and prospective customers, your target audience identified, a social media manager and your website is published and hosted. Now what?

Well, you might not know how to utilize the technology to get the results you need. You might run into trouble with a customer and think, "I could manage things *if* I had a better way of handling my existing and prospective customers and target audience." Your internet might stop working and you will think, "I could make use of this great equipment *if* I had good internet." There's always an *if!!* When you delay taking the next step because of the *ifs*, it is a clear sign that it is not your situation holding you back, but the fact that you are not ready to become an entrepreneur. That too is okay – just be sure to own it.

So, what's your story? Why have you decided to transition from a 9 to 5 employee working for an organization offering security, a solid paycheck on a weekly, bi-weekly or monthly basis, benefits, and no overhead to becoming an entrepreneur?

Perhaps the deciding factor for you in becoming an entrepreneur is that you are fed up with asking for permission to take a vacation, or permission to leave the office early due to a personal emergency. In your mind, the employer should have compassion for your own "personal" needs.

There is also feeling guilty about calling in sick for you or your children. In your mind, you are doing your employer a favor by showing up every day, working through lunch, and doing the work of two people for the same salary. So in essence, they should be lucky that you even show up every day, especially in bad weather, because you're the best employee that they have. *Is this the real reason you have decided to become an entrepreneur?*

Everybody has a starting point, and everybody has a

story, but there is nothing wrong with starting as an employee while you gather the information on your foundation.

It is however important to point out in all fairness to any business operation, that you do not want to utilize your employer's time while you search your own business opportunities. Please do not use the employer's devices and equipment, vendor connections, applications, time and energy; of which includes searching the internet. The employers are not paying you to pursue your own dreams, ventures and hopes of becoming an entrepreneur. There will be plenty of time (on your own time) to pursue and do the research... notice I emphasize the term *research*.

As you pursue being an entrepreneur, it is not always clear what's the step by step process to get there. Let's take you back to your educational years. In high school, you would have learnt about the historical and current business opportunities in blue collar, white collar corporate America, small business owners and partnerships.

But how would you begin to prepare for a business, even as a high school senior, ready to go off to college? Your actual journey can begin as you progress to higher education. At this point where adulthood begins, you are going to set the stages of your life with making those grown up decisions.

After graduation, do you work for someone or do you branch out on your own; do you work in corporate America, blue color jobs or build a business as an entrepreneur? You will start your research on Google for the estimated time of completion for each career choice.

You will have to ask yourself some serious questions. Are there processes I need to complete, and in any specific order? Who do you talk with about your career and/or business plans? A suggestion would be to start with your guidance counselors at the academic stages; where you will most likely be told first to do the research. We are taught those habits in school on the need to read tons of books, research, study hard and stay focused and study some more. You always needed to take plenty of notes, ask numerous questions as no question is a stupid question.

You are fully aware that the analysis is required; however, once you determine which industry you want to pursue, you want to be the subject matter experts in every facet of that industry. It is not only pinpointing the sector, but it must also address the industry's needs and requirements.

Your findings should encompass who wants or who meets that industry's needs and what are the roles and positions of the industry's end-users. If you plan to be a consultant, you must have those network connections and resources to assert that expertise. Although you may not have the immediate answer, you should know who to reach out to the get that answer. Those credible resources should be viable with certified credentials. Such resources have a stellar reputation and a sound history of success; including highly rated customer feedback and testimonials of taking their customers to the next level.

There are never too many questions you can ask. The only question that is unfortunate, is the question that is not being asked. If you do not ask you will never know, and ignorance is no excuse because there is a plethora of information available to you. The fact is, you must start the inquiries and discussions. You must also use your intuition, do the research and know right from the beginning to ask yourself – *"Is this for me?"*

In your research you may include network marketing opportunities within your specific industries of interest. Wherever there is a business platform, there is a network opportunity. This goes for most, if not all industries you desire to serve. And we cover networking opportunities more later in this book.

Again, it is not an overnight success, as every day in business we witness a rise and fall right before our eyes. We have witnessed the events in the news media, social media, and at your industry's current events and/or networking opportunities.

There are a number of factors to consider--for high school students, college students, those transitioning from the corporate world and looking to branch out on their own or those who are 9 to 5 considering the opportunities to go part time or do go full time - as a new entrepreneur.

This journey is REAL and not for everyone; so, let's take that journey together. In this book you will learn those specific actions you need to take. We will go step by step and outline exactly what you might encounter.

We will also cover the options that you have with those encounters and they will be in the back of the book. This will allow you to recap and take some additional notes, ask yourself some questions and fill in the blanks if you will, as you acquire the knowledge along this adventure. These measures can help you gage as to whether you are truly ready to be an entrepreneur because social media societies are not the end all…so do not believe the hype!!

CHAPTER 4

Research – Plan, EIN and D&B Number

The preparation and research needed during your discovery phase, whether it be with potential clients and/or investors is critical. Know where they have been and know their history. Know the status of their current state, and where they are going. Consider where you fit in, and how you could excel. What makes you better than your competitors, large or small? How can you take a company or your industry to the next level?

If you do not come in with resources, a network and expertise, then you know you are setting yourself up for failure. You must present and know your material. If you do not know the answer, acknowledge it and go back to the table with the answer and results. Remember that you are always, always, always a student. You are always learning something. If you stop learning, then you are in trouble, because an entrepreneur must keep learning.

Your industry is constantly evolving, and you must keep

up. Whether it is healthcare, IT, marketing, branding, etc., there is always a competitor. Well, apart from basket-weaving, but even that is being done by manufacturers. You must be the subject-matter expert in your field, so you are always growing.

Business Plan

Let's talk about the business plan, as an important thing to have as you start the process. Whether or not you know how to create a business plan, it is important to note that its content should outline your goals; and identify your target audience and the specific problems to solve, and how.

Your bio should clearly state why you are the best in the business to initiate and implement this plan, both long term or short term. The finance structure and distribution of funds should be specific. The business plan should also identify your resources for your market, both national and/or international.

Be sure to cover the physical structure of the business, as to whether it will be running out of your home, a brick and mortar online. The start-up cost should also include assets, salaries, compensation, cash, insurance and most importantly business taxes as these are key deciding factors in your planning.

The IRS well also help you "quickly" determine if your business is in fact a business or if it is a hobby. This will be based on your overall plan over at least a 5-year span, and the assets, liabilities, costs, revenue, losses and appropriate taxes to be paid, to which you should maintain quarterly accounts.

The key factors that must be included in your Start-Up Business Plan:

- Executive Summary
- General Business Description
- Products and Services
- Marketing Plan
- Operational Plan
- Management and Organization
- Personal Financial Statement
- Startup Expenses and Capitalization
- Financial plan
- Appendices
- Refining the Plan

Employer Identification Number (EIN)

There is also a need to apply for your employer identification number (EIN). An employer identification number (EIN) is a nine-digit number assigned by the IRS. It is used to identify the tax accounts of employers and certain other businesses who have no employees. The IRS uses the number to identify taxpayers who are required to file various business tax returns.

Data Universal Numbering System (D&B) Number

The D-U-N-S Number is a unique nine-digit identifier for businesses. It is used to establish a D&B business credit file, which is often referenced by lenders and potential business partners to help predict the reliability and/or financial stability of the business in question. D-U-N-S stands for data universal numbering system, is used to maintain up-to-date and timely information on more than millions of global businesses.

Let's talk about the research, which will be your primary contributor within your journey and those focal points will be noted in the proceeding chapters.

Research believe it or not, can determine if in fact this is truly something you want to pursue as a part-time or full-time entrepreneur. You are going to learn a lot of information and let me make it clear here, this is **not** a stage you want to rush through. It is also not a stage where you want to just grasp one component of your research and take off running; thinking it answers all questions.

When searching venues of your select industries of choice, that means you will be researching the latest and greatest business profile aspects. This includes the services provided, target audience, financials, successes and competitors, decision makers and staff.

Your research should clearly define which industry you want to pursue, and you are most passionate about whereas you find purpose and the need to serve.

CHAPTER 5

Research - Target Audience

The research on identifying your target audience begins with getting your questions documented and where to look for those answers. The measures along the way encounter pitfalls, to which you will learn at least in the beginning stages.

A solid foundation in this book will provide areas as to where to start, what to look for and who you should seek for those answers. This type of research could help to address where you intend to take your business, specific target audiences you are looking to reach and what problem are you trying to solve. Technically you are solving a problem your target audience has and will identify for you.

Start by characterizing your *Target Audience Avatars*--- Male/Female, Age, Stay @ home Parent, 9-5, College, HS Seniors, Corporate, Returning to Workforce Voluntary/Involuntary; Retirees/Widow/Widowers and the Industry Leaders and User You Want to Serve)

Pinpointing who is your target audience is critical. Not everyone is your target audience. So there will be individuals you will speak to or who will know your social media broadcasts – they are not all your target audience.

Your search for your target audience members needs to be precise, as you cannot simply just identify a target audience as *physicians* (i.e. What type of physician within a specific specialty or field of medicine; manufacturer of what type of product—automotive, retail, restaurant supplies, beauty industry-hair, make-up skin care etc.)

Are your target audience members' male, female, of a specific age range, race, religion or culture? Are they employed, unemployed stay at home parents, retirees returning to the workforce, employees with voluntary/involuntary termination transitioning between industries; College Grads heading out into the workforce; or executive leaders recently stepping down to pursue an entrepreneurship?

Keep in mind not all target audience members identified are your specific target audience members, and you may have one or have a few, but not all will apply to your service or product that you provide. Once you have identified your target audience now the work begins where you need to focus on their needs.

Your audience members will tell you what they need and it is very important that you do not push your agenda, but listen carefully to what they tell you the problem. You will have to present a product or service that applies to their specific needs. Reiterate in your business service proposal the specific issue to solve, how and what it will entail to successfully complete the task. Have thorough details on what your target audience members have identified; and who, what, when, where, why the issue and resolution is impactful. Be confident in your delivery on how you were going to solve their problem.

Know Ideal Your Customer

For example, my ideal customer would be a healthcare provider. People assume they have deep pockets, but even if they did not, healthcare providers tend to really value their customers since their customers are their patients. Healthcare providers value their team, too, and want to offer their best. They look to support and serve and offer the care that they took an oath to provide. That's my ideal customer. They work from the heart.

I have been blessed to have that type of customer. The money is the last thing they worry about when I bring them a proposal or, you know, when I consider my retainer agreement, the services I can provide to them, we save the money discussion for last. They want to know what they can do – and what I can do – to solve their problems. That's my ideal client. One who is receptive, who is ready to get the work done and who trusts me.

As you progress in acquiring that first contractual agreement with your new client, you too will use the social media venues and platforms to build on your target audience members and your followers too. Following the path of most social media influencers of integrity, you now will be in the role to present yourself as a subject matter expert, to which your target audience members will be watching, taking notes, posting comments and questions.

What is also important to consider, are the specific days and times your live broadcasts will be viewed by potential target audience members. It's a safe bet that if they are typically in operational work mode between 9 to 5, chances are they will not be watching a live broadcast that you presented social media. They can always watch a replay, but the live broadcast scheduling will allow them to have that virtual time with you and obtain quick real-time Q&A. But even watching the replays, your viewers can always post their questions and comments, and it is very important that you respond timely to keep them engaged and the momentum up.

You will find that not all followers, target audience members or community members of your industry congregate in the same social media venues. Some you may find on Facebook, Instagram, LinkedIn, and even on Pinterest, just to name a few. It is important that you understand where they reside most, as some may have one media platform or a couple. Using hashtags (#) followed by the industry name of choice (i.e. #healthcaretechnology) on each social media site will provide a vast account of where the audience members go to most.

The goal is to get to know your audience members, your target audience members, and your followers on a more personal basis but do not confuse the two. For instance, you may have a prospective client who enjoys fishing or art, so you may find a Pinterest board page where he or she displays their personal postings of artwork or fishing expeditions, so that will give you a "personal" edge on customer relations and perhaps an advantage to acquiring a new client.

Networking opportunities can even be found on Pinterest, if your research and diligence is persistent and thorough.

CHAPTER 6

Research – Social Media Influencers

Your social media platform will be a benefit to as an entrepreneur. It is an opportunity for you as an entrepreneur to present yourself as the expert in your field. As you become a social media influencer yourself, you will be setting the stage and outlining an effective path to build a following. You will also be able to network with industry leaders and others so that you want capitalize on researching your industry and competitors.

It is important to remember that social media is not necessarily your sole entity of interest where you will acquire some questions asked and answered.

You can use social media to post your own engaging comments to social media posts and live broadcasts; to seek out feedback and reactions from your audience.

You will hear the term target audience. Target audiences are those women, men, young women, and young men of a different calibers to be considered a target audience, based on your plan of action and industry line you intend to serve with your business plans.

Be careful of the extensive time, energy and investments made towards these influencers. Be mindful of their agendas and those that follow them as well. You have heard the phrase, *birds of a feather*? Be diligent in your discovery on their specific platforms and any/all products and services they offer.

Do not be surprised if while watching the live broadcast of these social media influencers that their products and services that they promote can range from $197 up to $2700; and it's important to point out that those are the *sale* prices not their normal prices.

Now here is another one of those *pause* moments, in the real-world aka in person, you would be a little leery at simply giving an unknown presenter your credit or debit card or writing them a check without doing some research first. This is the age of technology -quick fast and in a hurry.

You'll hear the phrase you can pay by PayPal, Stripe or by CashApp, but you must pay by midnight tonight or it will go back up to the regular price. I think it is a safe bet that in the real world you would casually be making your way to the back of the room and then to the right as you exit the room because you are not feeling so secure about paying for a service you haven't really researched or done your homework. Nor do you know the presenter that you can trust that she is truly the expert in her field, can speak on the topic at hand and that you'll learn anything at all from her. What do you get for your dollar and in this case between $197 up to $2700 and even more, if you wait until after midnight.

I circle back to the reference *"do not believe the hype"* because currently such influencers bank on the fast and accelerated pace of their products and service purchases and the heighten marketing pitch that if you do not move quickly, you will be left behind…forever! Not so and not so fast!

In addition to looking at online search behavior, it's important to look at what people are saying about your brand – and whether the conversation is moving in a positive or negative direction.

Notice we're still on the topic of *research*. Who is this social media influencer that has caught your attention as a subject matter expert that you believe may have the answers and the followers that resemble your target audience? Have you read any of their books, have you attended any of their speaking engagements, have you registered and participated in any of their online webinars? Have you heard their podcast; have you completed a full discovery as to who they are, where they are located, their background and history in your industry, or the industry they claim to be an expert in?

Who can validate and support the credentials of your newfound influence? Those that may tell you your credentials or your degrees do not matter, "do not believe that hype" or in that case…nonsense. That is because *their* credentials and *their* degrees need to be validated because they perhaps found no worth or value in the education and training and research within the industry that they chose.

When it comes to determining your target audience's needs and what content you need to bring to the table, with regard to what services or products you need to provide, credentials education, training, certification requirements, technology, maintenance, security, upgrades and cutting-edge resources are contributing factors. The results from your thorough research, your competitor feedback and your audience members themselves will confirm what your credentials and education must entail in order to proceed to the next level.

You will find social media influencers who proclaim to be 6 or 7 figure earners and that they have clients who are 6 and 7 figure earners. However, there is a term we often use and that is "Receipts" meaning there is proof that can be presented or has been presented upon request and you have witnessed the proof of these receipts based on the live broadcasts many of them will conduct in order to authenticate the results of their efforts with working with a social media influencer. These are the type of social media influencers you need to follow, and that may include their receipt-holding followers. But keep in mind, they have put in the work and reap the rewarding results.

Their research and education, course content, support

and validation are all in order. Accountability and integrity are critical as an entrepreneur and you must complete the work, your BEST work. Be accountable, hold your staff and clients accountable, hold your vendors and resources accountable; as you have chosen to transition from *comfortable* part-time or full-time 9 -5 employee to the world of entrepreneurship.

CHAPTER 7

Research – Vendors, Innovation & Stability

Your research should also include thorough reviews on the vendors for your industry and who are the top vendors or the vendors of choice for your industry. Again, your research on your target audiences will give you that information. Be sure to capture data on their:

- successes and their failures
- strengths and weakness
- history of turn-around times
- revenue
- their status in the industry are they credentialed
- certifications
- existing and prospective customers'/target audience
- credibility their existing and prospective customers and competitors in the industry

As the entrepreneur, you would be considered as a subject matter expert on vendors and the go-to resource for your customer. Your target audience will need and seek your expertise as to the best options. Always provide the clients with a *minimum* of three of the top performing vendor that support the clients' operations.

Be sure you have completed a thorough review of the vendors' services and product lines; which includes customer testimonials and a comparison of the vendor's pricings, product and service lines and their major clientele.

It is important as the subject matter expert, to never give your customer just one vendor selection as that sends red flags that there might be a possible conflict of interest. Take into consideration that if the client has been in business for a long time, rest assured they have done their research too on vendor statuses. Clients complete marketing research as well, and are in the business for profit, longevity and success. They are very interested in your specific findings as a leading entrepreneur seeking their business. In fact, your research results are more credible then theirs and have more foundation and selection substance to meet that criteria.

The vendors that support each operational need begins registration. These are the main factors that impact an organization's revenue and success. Maintain notes on all facets of your industry and you do not want to miss those opportunities, as they evolve.

Again, I mention revenue which is basically the bottom line depending on your industry . What are the revenue aspects? What are you trying to accomplish? So you'll spend a lot of time in this area. No question is a silly question but they should all be addressed.

I'll give you a helpful hint. If you want to know what those questions are in the industry, for instance if you want to go into network marketing then try LinkedIn. Go and look for those memberships.

You'll find that you'll need a personal Facebook page and a business page. Do not confuse the two. Always keep those two separate and as far as your business page and business research, ask the question if you were to have a new opportunity to get complete software for your offices, what would be your vendor of choice?; or what would be your device of choice.

Your audience will tell you if you are picking the correct models to finance. For instance they will tell you the best, the latest, and the greatest software and resources, and which one of the network events you need to connect to.

Your audience will tell you what they want, and they will tell you what they need. Because they are giving you that information does not mean they know where to get it. I know what I want, but I may not know where to get it. Your job is to hear what they need and to take note of that.

I am not saying that that social media is the only place to get your answer. There are multiple venues you have to check, because you would be asking for a crash and burn by using only one resource. You can get those same questions answered using uncle Google.

Post your questions and challenges in the search field, to seek the preference on the latest and greatest finance industry resources and software and much more. Specific topics in areas of interest are highly sought after in your industry and its target audience well make that plain for you, by posting good and bad reviews, testimonies and specific examples as to why this is a need that would be an opportunity for you to meet as an entrepreneur.

Financing for Start-Up Businesses

Is it a hobby or a business? The IRS can determine that for you and we will talk about that later. But that's another opportunity for you to research the history and is it long term or short term or is its overnight success of a fly by night fad?

A small business start-up loan is explicitly designed towards start-ups with little to no business history. There are an array of small business start-up loans and financing methods available to new business owners—from SBA micro-loans, business credit, friends and family to GoFundMe.

These options present specific pros and cons, depending on your financing needs, ability to repay the loan and the strength of your credit scores, based on the utilization of your social security number (SSN) or established EIN.

Pros

- Great option for new businesses with a limited financial history
- Interest-free for first 9 to 15 months

- No prepayment penalty
- Only a credit report needed for pre-approval and no secured deposit

Cons

- Can take 30 to 45 days to complete the financing process
- Functions as a high-limit credit card, not as cash
- Exceptional credit required

For businesses in operation for less than six months, it is typically suggested to pursue one small business start-up loan options. Businesses in operation for six months or more could have more traditional business loan offerings and should consider applying for those instead.

Your financing eligibility for more alternative small business start-up financing options like grants, sponsorships, crowdfunding, or friends and family will be less influenced by your credit score and more on the details of your business plan, of which we covered previously in detail.

CHAPTER 8

Research – Competitors as Resourceful Rivals

It is important that you know your competitors. First, because many of your own strengths come naturally to you, so you do not always realize you have them. Knowing your competitors' weaknesses may help you identify your strengths. It is extremely important for you to know about the positioning, pricing, strengths, and weaknesses of your competitors. Awareness of your competitors will help you to communicate with your target audience, distinguish your business from competitors, improve your processes, and navigate challenges in your market.

There is no shame, and there is no fault in researching your rivals because trust and believe, those competing in your industry have done the research and are examining you as well. I do not want to sugarcoat this as some of them may not be so cooperative and that is okay too, but your job is still to know the difference between the two.

Your clients or prospective clients may have also made some additional attempts and reached out to gather vendor and competing for information-- to make sure they are getting the most bang for their buck. This tactic occurs many times, just before a client agrees to a contractual agreement for your services.

These preparation measures are a part of the process, so always stay on top of your industry needs, the cutting-edge technology innovations and growth opportunities upon the entrepreneurial horizon. From what your competitors are doing, you may find that you all will exchange opportunities; meaning that they may have a client that has a need they cannot fulfill but are assured you can.

As a competing resource, you provide the same professional courtesy. Such collaborative efforts show the rivalry as professional and resourceful and win-win for the client. Competing entrepreneurs work together because mature entrepreneurs collaborate, they do not compete.

These results are win-win for the clients, and a significant benefit because they have the best of both worlds. The clients would have the best in the industry working collectively to get the optimal result. From a client's perspective, this is a success, not a threat and a benefit with perks that we identified about earlier.

There are such perks along the way, and again this is part of your network because you are among those competing in your industry. Consider the build of your own networking platform, as those examples are vital components.

There are strategic bonuses believe it or not to pursuing this journey with integrity, validation, trust and respect from existing and prospective customers; including those deemed your competitive resources. It is a major compliment to have the respect from your existing client, past clients and truly that of the competitors in your industry.

The competitive resources pose additional opportunities for you. It positions strength, prompts you to think outside the box; and rivalry provides an opportunity for collaboration. I have collaborated with many in my industry.

On the outside, you are looking at them as a competitor; however, we know more about each other and our businesses then our own clients or even our family members. When they know that you share the same professional business realm, that too becomes part of the research. Again, pay close attention to what you should be observing and acknowledging to which you can leverage as an advantage. This is not an overnight process and you need to do the research on your competitors who will be your allies; but it is a friendly competition.

These strategies will enable you to set your prices competitively and provide a response to rival marketing campaigns with your business initiatives. Create marketing strategies that make the most of your competitors' weaknesses and advance your business performance.

Actively monitor and assess any threats posed by both

new contributing and current competitors to your industry market. With amplified use of the robust Internet to shop and purchase products and services and to find places to go, you are no longer just competing with your brick and mortars. You will discover you are competing with businesses from a global scale as well, with global venues and opportunities that are booming. Listed below are channels of existing competitors:

- Local and state business directories
- Local Chambers of Commerce
- Cable, Social Media and Newspaper Advertising
- Press Releases
- Exhibitions and Trade Fairs
- Surveys
- Internet Searches for comparable Products or Services
- Information shared by existing and prospective customers and target markets
- Sales flyers/banners and marketing sources received by list building methods – very common marketing tactic
- Thorough research required for existing patented products and/or trademarks on intellectual property—**critical step**
- Planning presentations and developing works underway

There are (2) distinct competitors, direct competitors of whom offer the same product or services and indirect competitors of whom sustain the same products and services; but utilize unconventional methods.

"Get the buzz" on your competitors, both current and up and coming. Speak to your competitors. Contact them by phone, email or fax and ask for a copy of their brochure or get one of your staff or a friend to drop by and pick up their marketing literature. Competitors are business driven as well, so do not be surprised if your "survey team member(s)" are asked for their contact information, or if they would like to meet with a consult. I typical reply, *"Let me review the material first and should I have any questions, I will definitely call you or stop in again."*

Always, always ask for a detailed price listing and inquire about the vendor's mass-produced item costs and what the discount is for high volume purchases. This negotiation will pinpoint which items a competitor will discount and at what volume.

Believe it or not, your competitors thrive on the interaction with their competing colleagues. Maintain both phone and face-to-face contacts so you stay in tune to their class of the business, the quality of their published content and the initial brand impact made with existing and prospective customers and target market.

There is no doubt you will meet or reconnect with competitors at social and business events. Do not avoid them, greet and mingle. Be approachable – they are your competing colleagues, not your enemies. It is also very likely that you will need each other one day, for example in collaborating to grow a new market for a new product; or transitioning new or existing clientele, based on their operational needs; but keep in mind, this is still a win-win!

Be sure to listen carefully to your existing and prospective customers, target market and suppliers; and not force your own views and opinion.

Study and always work to optimize your business model in relation to the competition; of which will broaden your knowledge about your target audience and industry so that you can refine your business strategies, as your industry and customer needs evolve.

The status term *competitors positioning* is also noteworthy for future reference, as it means an array of settings or conditions under which a business stages its offering is its positioning. This is key information business owners should know about your competitors.

Monitor the way your competitors do business. Observe the:

- Products or services provided and how they market them to existing and prospective customers and target market
- Pricing plans
- Method of distribution and delivery
- Hardware and/or software employed to optimize customer loyalty and support the product and service offerings
- Branding and rebranding design values

- Innovation – business services and/or product methods
- Staffing tallies and the competence of staff recruits
- IT Utilization – Internet and Email Marketing/List Building
- Identify the Business Owners and View their Credentialing Profiles
- Annual report – Public Business applies
- Active media activities - check their website, social media platforms as well as local newspapers, radio, television and billboards/marques

The target audience of your competitors are also of focus point that you be taken into consideration Do they influence to an age group, gender, financial status or niche market? Are they a cutting-edge service or geared for the cost-conscious? Do they use environmentally friendly services or products? The more knowledgeable about your competitors' positioning, the more robust you can optimize your own.

The consequences of failing to compete on value will be worse: chaotic, costly care of uneven quality, with a growing toll on individuals and the economy. Real competition **must** be the course forward. Businesses that try to deflect competition are on the wrong side of history and the wrong side of strategy.

As competition is par for the course, the ultimate goals you are to provide the very best products and service offerings to your existing and prospective customers and target market for long-term success. This determines a competitor's strength.

With our weaknesses, we are all work in progress, and knowing our own areas of improvement, you should also know the weaknesses of your competitors. Having the knowledge of your competitors' weaknesses can assist with you as an entrepreneur identify you and your business strengths, as their weakness must build upon your areas for improvement.

Incorporate those found weaknesses in your competitors into a new strength for your own business those gaps and areas for improvement are opportunities that should not be taken lightly, and you should move aggressively and thoroughly to optimize all potential areas of new business opportunities.

There are always lessons learned from your research of your competitors' platforms. Maintain active profiles on those areas, to improve your areas or expertise and add increased value to your business, clients and prospective clients within your target market.

If you are certain your competitors are executing a product or service better than you, do not rush to the drawing board, do the research and confirm if in fact there is a market for the product or service, or if in fact it is simply a break/fix incident, to which you could have solve; opposed to reinventing a wheel that had no growing market for. It could be anything from improving customer service, assessing your pricing plans, updating your products or services or marketing plans and materials; and even rebranding yourself, redesigning your website and shifting your suppliers.

To get a more accurate picture of how your competitors are shaping up, below are some further suggestions:

- First and foremost, this is also an optimal time for self-evaluation Are they getting more publicity than you, perhaps through networking or sponsoring events?
- Attend trade shows, local and national conferences. An excellent opportunity to examine competitors' products and services. This includes their traffic volumes.
- Study the annual reports of your competitors, usually available for download from their websites. If a public business, as required.
- Initiate communication with their former employees. If a competitor has a high employee turnover or staff laying offs, you can gain firsthand internal knowledge. Be mindful of a hidden and perhaps a bitter agenda, with the receipt of extensive information to benefit your business plans.
- Scan the jobs advertisements. Jobs on offer and their descriptions are often good indicators of changes in your competitors' strategies or organizational structures.
- *Business* websites frequently provide extensive information that has not traditionally been revealed -

from the history of the business to biographies of the staff.
- Use search engines to track down similar products. Find out who else offers them and how they go about it.
- Check their "interactive sections" on the site for areas where you can improve on your business website. Is the information free of charge, if not, are the fees reasonable, too high or too low? Is it easy to find and navigate through?
- Websites can give you lead commands on what businesses that are located locally, nationally and internationally are accomplishing in your industry sector.
- Check the competitor's entries in public and professional directories. If they are an online business, ask for a trial of their service.

Try to innovate not imitate. With brainstorming ideas, always verify if can you do it even better, add more value. Your competitors might not have rights over their actual brainstorming ideas, but recall the rules on patents, copyright, trademark and design rights.

Customer service reputation can often provide the authentication between businesses that operate in a very competitive market. Renew your efforts in these areas to manipulate the deficiencies you have discovered via your competitors.

Never be complacent about your current strengths.

Current product and service offerings with your own business may still need improving, and as a result, competitors may also be assessing your business offerings, to which they could implement and enhance.

Keep in mind based on the up's and downs of your industries, you and/or your competitors may endure a weakness or challenge of a significant nature due to a common problem or issue that has transpired within your industry, community, or target market. As you and your competitors haring countering the same challenges it is very important that you keep abreast and informed as to how those challenges are being handled by your competitors and how they are avoiding those risk and challenges.

Check out the rankings of your competitors' websites, locally, nationally and internationally. Their web analytic data can also be captured on how a website performs overall, such as updates, network connections, interfaces, engagement rates, avatars, per each visit, including the duration, date and time zone.

Identify the opportunities and locations they may investing in online marketing efforts via "high traffic" data and purchasing histories.

What do your competitor existing and prospective customers and target market find appealing about them? Although your business offerings meet the industry's needs, you may wish to expand and monopolize the market with products and service offerings, in a mass effort to win them over. The goal is always to produce the most positive customer experience possible.

However, there may be some things that your competitors offer that you won't be able to match or exceed. In this case, it will not be worth your time or effort to try and win existing and prospective customers and target market over in this area. Your business can't meet every need, and that is perfectly okay. Now you know where your time and energy will be best spent.

Even when momentum and/or demand is low, businesses should not pursue is consolidation that does not directly lead to improved value for patients. there is a competitive opportunity both to redesign care delivery so that it improves value. Organizations that are hungry or troubled —are often the most innovative, generating new choices and stimulating competition.

In addition, sign up to receive Google Alerts via email so whenever or wherever your competitors are covered by media or bloggers online, you can stay up-to-date on when they launch new products or when the business is receiving positive or negative press.

You need to strive to take hold in your industry, decision makers at every level need real choices, for example in healthcare: consumers when selecting health insurance products, patients when choosing clinicians, and clinicians when selecting the facilities where their patients receive care.

Consequently, you should know what both your

competitors' strengths and weaknesses are. It is extremely important for you to know about the positioning, pricing, strengths, and weaknesses of your competitors. The insights you gather on your industry and your own business will help you to improve your marketing strategies and truly stand out to your target audience.

CHAPTER 9

Product, Service Selection and Pricing

Entrepreneurs should always be familiar with their competitors' pricing for many reasons. The first reason would be so that you can keep your pricing align with what consumers in your target market are willing to pay. Study and acquire education about new pricing modules that are more appealing to existing and prospective customers and target market.

Awareness of your competitors' pricing does not suggest that your pricing can match or surpass theirs. The primary point is to understand where your pricing falls in comparison to your competitors in the vast market. Lower pricing points would be considered an advantage. The challenge, especially in a small business market would be to convince prospective clients that the value of your product or service is as good, if not better than as those with higher pricing.

The alternate challenge would be if your price plans are higher than that of your competitors, of which means you will need to indicate the significant benefits that accompany your pricing. It is not uncommon for target markets and/or loyal existing and prospective customers to switch to a competitor if the price is low enough, so your sales pitch should capture their attention with a primary advantage as to the reason to pay more. Pitch it, "you get what you pay for."

Familiarizing yourself with your competitors pricing will help you strategically position the pricing that is ideal for your business and reap the benefit of acquiring and retaining existing and prospective customers and target market with those prices.

Optimize your customer interactions with your existing and prospective customers and target market. Do not simply ask how your business is performing - ask which of your competitors they are familiar with if any, and how your entity parallels. Customers are also more inclined to share, in you create a comfort environment. Have lunch catered or perhaps host a vendor of their choice…and remember the refreshments!

Use meetings with your suppliers to ask what their other existing and prospective customers and target market are doing. They may not tell you everything you want to know, but a strategic starting point.

Use your judgment with any content shared freely. For instance, when existing and prospective customers and target market say your prices are higher than the competition they may just be trying to negotiate a better deal.

CHAPTER 10

Invest in Yourself and Your Legacy – No Discounts

Emerging entrepreneurs often begin their journey solo, serving every function in their new businesses, and not even entertaining the thought of staffing (on-site or virtual). Deeming themselves as the brainstorm community, the zealous leaders, the team builders, engineers, analysts, marketing authorities, logistics officers, accountants and strategists combined.

The reality is that repeatedly this stage is required. What that implies is that one of the most challenging factors for the emerging entrepreneur to do, is to keep investing and building both their personal and professional skills and competences.

Time, resources and focus drivers are an epic challenge for the emerging entrepreneurs and this includes entrepreneurs needing to "level up" their industry statuses. Most entrepreneurs bypass the essential investments since those investments appear detached from their businesses, products and services. If an entrepreneur has an extra hour, for example, he or she many prefer to invest in their business above investing in their own personal development areas.

The primary point overlooked with this mindset or approach is that most entrepreneurs are in fact their brands, products and services. Since your entire entrepreneurial venture rests on a single set of shoulders, it makes business sense to ensure that those shoulders are as prepared, as skilled and as strong as possible.

It is important that you always keep your ears and eyes open, as our industries evolve. Perhaps the platform of your current employer or employer of choice is where you want to start. In healthcare-IT for example, if you wish to pursue and stay in that industry and to expand your knowledge for your business then perhaps becoming a consultant for technology or consultant for the clinical aspects of health care. There is a piece of the puzzle or opportunity for everyone to expand their own horizons beyond imagination.

There is always, always a professional membership that you should connect with and one opportunity is on LinkedIn. Check out LinkedIn and the professional membership associations that represent the industries both you and your prospective clients are affiliated with.

You want to make sure the entities are nationally accredited; and should you decide to join (great idea), there are annual memberships fees and hosted conferences and events. It is imperative to oblige and build your knowledge, expertise and expand on networking opportunities. Once you get your foot in the door, do not be a lurker, observer or unapproachable…mingle, introduce yourself to other attendees (do not sit by yourself), meet the sponsors and vendors, make a few solid connections, network…network!!

I strongly encourage you to research those particular memberships, as some of them are private groups to which require certain criteria; and others are groups where they can share and collaborate. You will also see a lot of questions and answers and/or just some venting about observations that have been made.

You will learn a great deal from these memberships, and strategic networking within your industry's memberships is vital. There is always a buzz on innovative technology updates, so you want to make sure to stay informed on latest and greatest technology meeting your industry's needs.

You will spend a great deal amount of time and energy into the research and you will be checking multiple venues. Uncle Google is not the only sole place to get your information; however, there is credible content on the internet, books, magazines, podcasts, blogs etc.

Your thorough research will provide answers; but, what I need to make clear is that you should not just use one primary sole source. Your countless sources may include a mentor in your select industry, a referral; or business coach that can work with one on one in a virtual setting or person to person.

Just in case you were wondering, the answer is yes,

business coaches can work with you virtually via platforms such as Zoom or Skype. Your mentors may be national or international, but here again do your research on their credentials as well; before any contract is signed and any coaching fees are paid.

You may discover business coaches in other states, or outside your specific industry; yet that is OK, as the main factor to consider is if they know the primary stages of business. Business coaches from various industries have trained and groomed millions of employees (i.e. 9-5'ers and/or transitioning) and entrepreneurs throughout their journey towards entrepreneurship.

Mentors and business coaches can share their paths with you, to which you will be able to pay-it-forward to others who may seek your expertise. Because one way or the other you'll be able to take this information and share with others who will also pursue the area of becoming an entrepreneur or finding out based on all the research whether not this is a step but they want to take.

But again it is not a step that you want to rush through Be thorough and be diligent. Definitely seek those who were in the industry. People love for you to pick their brain. They love to mentor and want to answer your questions as they won't consider that a threat.

The two key components that you will find with many if not all entrepreneurs are their passion and their purpose. This is what drives that momentum and gets them up early in the morning and plenty of late nights.

It is basically referred to as a 110% grind mode to make their dreams possible, to make it successful and build a platform to pass down to their legacies. Your investment should be in long-term opportunities to you want to leave behind for your legacy.

CHAPTER 11

Negatives and Positives to Being an Entrepreneur

The positives would include flexibility with the work schedule and the abundance of education and training. You just need to love learning new things and, in our industries, something is always evolving. Something is always changing. As soon as you get one product released, within 90 days to a year, you have an upgrade. You must stay just above the cutting edge and get your customers in the right positions. The networking is another positive, and more control over your compensation.

The negatives would include the fact that as an entrepreneur, you cannot turn off that grind. You go to bed with it. It is in your dreams. It is probably the first thing you wake up to because your laptop, your iPad or your cell phone are lying by your head. People often use the term "work-life balance," but I disagree with that. I do not think there's a work-life balance. One of the two must be a sacrifice. As an entrepreneur, it is generally your personal or family life.

I know we do not want to face that, but it's true. It is a sacrifice. You are late to the games. You are late to the family dinners, if in fact you make them at all. There is also a contradiction in the work schedules. It might be a challenging customer that you have, and you can't turn around and blame it on the boss because you are the boss. So now what? You are the one with all the hats, and that could probably be a negative.

Entrepreneurs and aspiring entrepreneurs will encounter each other at conferences and vendor-sponsored events. Utilize these opportunities to mingle and have breakfast or lunch with them. These networking events allow you the chance exchange some ideas, toss business your way, or feel you out on what you are doing to meet the needs of your existing and prospective customers and target market.

Competing rivals will often exchange some challenges that they are encountering and seek your input and vice versa. Again, there is nothing wrong with that, and that is par for the course; as well as it is part of your research trait of the networking. Do the work and what is necessary, gain the knowledge because you do not want to be out here by yourself, nor do you have to be.

Continue to strive for that extra pull, as you wish that supplemental opportunity to become a more resourceful subject matter expert. As an entrepreneur, you will be deemed a subject matter expert. Subject matter experts are always learning, so when I speak of research, you will still be engaged in some form of study and research within the industry field you intend to serve.

I could be talking to the choir right now as target audience members of this book (i.e., high school, college, adults transitioning back into the workforce or switching careers to increase skill sets); however, you must realize that this journey will require work, time, attention, focus, and sacrifice.

Technology alone changes every day, and there is always another opportunity for optimized software and hardware devices - it never changes. The consistent research never ends, and that is my first point - do the work. It is not an overnight result, as it will be ongoing, so make a note of that in your records "research will be ongoing."

There are network opportunities where its membership programs will also provide the opportunities even as college students to join these membership organizations for the fields in healthcare, technology, marketing, finance, manufacturing or coaching and consulting.

Either an entrepreneur is in business for themselves or clients needing your expertise with consultation services to get them to the next level, and you will have that information. Your primary tasks should be to pursue what are the needs, wants and opportunities that your industry requires.

Also, making sure that it outlines the actual location settings with the real estate, down to the complete office set-up. Staff educational needs should be addressed, and the content must focus on the client's operational requirements, and staff roles and their levels of expertise.

Additionally, the time and cost for the staff training that will be required, and pricing may vary, based their knowledge, maintenance for compliance and new staff recruitments. Your results will be very beneficial, both in the long term and short term, as you show the clients that you too have a vested interest in the success of their business operations and staff development.

CHAPTER 12

Rinse and Repeat Entrepreneurial Journey Q & A

In one paragraph, Define an Employee to Entrepreneur Journey

_____
_____
_____
_____
_____
_____
_____

What is Your Specific Story?

_____
_____
_____
_____
_____
_____

_____
_____
_____
_____
_____

Name (11) Key Factors to Include in a Business Plan?

1)
2)
3)
4)
5)
6)
7)
8)
9)
10)
11)

Do You Know How to Obtain an Employer Identification Number (EIN)?

_____
_____
_____

Do You Know How to Obtain a D&B Number?

_____
_____
_____

What constitutes you target audience? Is everyone considered your target market, if so how? If not, why?

_____
_____
_____
_____
_____
_____
_____

Why is research a critical factor with starting a business; in studying your competitors and promoting your products and service offers?

_____
_____
_____
_____
_____
_____
_____

Name (11) Ways to Monitor the Way Your Competitors Do Business:

    1)
    2)
    3)
    4)
    5)

6)
7)
8)
9)
10)
11)

What Government Entity and At What Point Is It Determined That Your Business is Ultimately a Hobby and Not a Business?

-
-

Name (3) Workflow Steps in the Discovery Phase-

1)
2)
3)

Name (3) Methods an Entrepreneur Can Invest in Themselves-

1)
2)
3)

Name (3) Take-Aways From Researching Social Media Influencers-

1)

2)
3)

Why is learning your competitors' strategies for pricing their products and services important?

_____
_____
_____
_____
_____
_____
_____

CONCLUSION

In a nutshell, an individual need to have a driven entrepreneurial characteristic and first-class personal qualities to become a successful entrepreneur.

Specifically, the entrepreneur behaviors are networking, transparent risk taker, observant, visionary, failure is an option, transparent culture, result-oriented, team-oriented and proactive to exhibit an excellent entrepreneur. These entrepreneur characteristics are the main values that need to be studied, followed and applied by all seeking this status.

To become a success is due to these attributes and will determine the success or failure of small or corporate business development, which also determines whether the formation of core competitiveness of enterprises. These entrepreneur traits can be ranked as essential factors that differ the difference between the successful entrepreneur and the common entrepreneur. The most successful entrepreneurs in the world practice and apply at least one, if not most of these behaviors.

Nonetheless, successful entrepreneurs are the motivation and catalyst of the economic pillars in the country. Our countries cannot not reach or excel the level of more developed countries if there are no successful entrepreneurs building those masses as they are the backbone of economic development.

Today, communities can no longer expect large enterprises to guarantee them jobs for life. Entrepreneurs are increasingly expected to seek out their own opportunities, actively create value and perform ethically, be authentic rather than dependably follow rules and routines set by others.

High school and college students need to learn to be enterprising, both when working for others and when setting up their own businesses. Being innovative involves taking responsibility for decision making enterprise-wide, becoming increasingly self-reliant, ground-breaking, risk-taking, audacious, dynamic, progressive, opportunist, ambitious and sustaining your values, as well as being able to initiate ideas and see them through into action.

Assembling the right questions and that starts with knowing the type of business you want to pursue, whether you actually want to start your own business. Let me point out there is nothing wrong with becoming and remaining a 9 to 5 employee. We have all done it and started somewhere. I flipped burgers myself.

I hope that sharing my insights of this realistic journey, will alleviate you also to go from being just employed to an entrepreneur.

Be Unemployable…It's a Game Changer!

ABOUT THE AUTHOR

JEWEL D. KITKO, MHA, CLSSGB, CHTS-IM

Jewel is a Michigan native from the Metropolitan Detroit area, a mom and phenomenal grandma of 2, and now resides in Fort Lauderdale, FL.

She has a Bachelor's degree in Health Information Management (BS), a Masters in Health Administration (MHA), and Associate Degree in Health Information Technology. Jewel is also a Certified Lean Six Sigma Green Belt, Registered Health Information Administrator (RHIA), and Certified Healthcare Technology Specialist - Implementation Manager (CHTS-IM).

As the Founder and CEO of Diamond HIT Consult LLC, Jewel is a certified Health-IT Implementation Manager and has provided successful results in private physician and ambulatory practices to restructure and transition to more efficient operations.

Jewel has been able to go from being just an employee to an entrepreneur. Jewel's mission has proven results that impact thousands of national and international healthcare professionals with certified HIT innovations and workflows that increase patient volumes, quality of care and surpass revenue goals.

Jewel's primary mission is to keep God first and foremost and prepare a legacy for her children. She is committed to serving as a health services executive leader, living a healthy and balanced life, applying ethical principles to every area of her life and inspiring others through her physical and written works.

    Jewel is elated with her entrepreneurship and networking with some phenomenal industry leaders and other entrepreneurs – along the way of her own journey and success. Jewel hopes that sharing her insights of this realistic journey, will alleviate you also to go from being just employed to an entrepreneur.

www.jewelkitko.com
Instagram.com/jewelkitko
Facebook.com/jewel.kitko
Linkedin.com/in/jeweldkitko
Twitter.com/jewelkitko

www.ingramcontent.com/pod-product-compliance
Lightning Source LLC
Chambersburg PA
CBHW071424220526

45469CB00004B/1416